Scars of a Boy Soldier

Alex Olango

Published by New Generation Publishing in 2016

Copyright © Alex Olango 2016

First Edition

The author asserts the moral right under the Copyright, Designs and Patents Act 1988 to be identified as the author of this work.

All Rights reserved. No part of this publication may be reproduced, stored in a retrieval system or transmitted, in any form or by any means without the prior consent of the author, nor be otherwise circulated in any form of binding or cover other than that which it is published and without a similar condition being imposed on the subsequent purchaser.

www.newgeneration-publishing.com

New Generation Publishing

Dedication

My beloved dad, you fell a victim, may your death find justice.

Mother, my siblings, Norah, Di
I dedicate this book to you.

To all the victims of the atrocities committed, let's all hope for peace and recovery in Northern Uganda.

Acknowledgements

I choose to acknowledge the people of Northern Uganda, those who are still suffering from the wrath of their own son of the soil.

To those who lost their loved ones due to the insurgency, may their souls rest in eternal peace.

To those who are still waiting on the Lord to bring back their sons, their daughters and their friends, and to the fallen heroes, I salute you wherever you are.

This story is not only mine; it's also a story of more than 30,000 other innocent children abducted by the LRA, like me.

Contents

Chapter 1: Village childhood 1
Chapter 2: Night commuting 12
Chapter 3: Abduction 15
Chapter 4: Crossing the river 21
Chapter 5: Opoka 26
Chapter 6: Tinka 29
Chapter 7: To Sudan 31
Chapter 8: JuJu 39
Chapter 9: Sudan... 51
Chapter 10: Escape 60
Chapter 11: Leopards.. 63
Chapter 12: Coming home 67

Introduction to my story

In this book, I attempt the most difficult walk of my life. I can't find a destination. Not to take it that far, I don't have a direction.

I am going to take you into my life from zero background, to freedom. Read as I struggle with life and nightmares, feel, admire and hate the people I met on the way.

This is who I am.

The suffering of others, those who are still trapped in the lion's den, those who returned but found out there was no need because there wasn't anyone to return to and those parents still waiting for their children to miraculously show up after being gone 20 years should concern me, should concern you. There is indeed a global need to continue to bring support and solidarity to those suffering from a total denial of basic rights.

I have been so much tormented by the magnitude of torture that I and the other children went through. I have gone through a series of physical and psychological traumas with which, without help, I'm not sure what would have become of me.

Already I have suffered more than my ancestors. I am so proud of the things I have done and if I am fortunate enough to achieve the things I always strived for, I will continue fighting until I break the locks. I am prepared to surmount any obstacles lying between me and peace in Northern Uganda.

I am afraid each time I pick up a pen to write a line, but I am more afraid for the people who feature in the scripts. Therefore, at some point, the few names used aren't real, for security purposes, because these Nazis are still romping in our land. I can't risk their lives or mine because there is a chance of re-abduction. I could get killed and they could get killed. I want the characters in this book to be free from danger. That's the reason I chose to make the ordinary people in this book anonymous.

The leaders' names are well known.

Some parts of the book lack dialogue just because I was 11 and 12 years of age when most of the things happened to me. The prima-facie evidences of the tortures are still seen up to now, both emotionally and physically – my various scars of a boy soldier.

After I escaped the war, at the rehabilitation centre, I must say that I never slept. I was only thinking and scared whenever nights fell. I was afraid of any army uniform around the centre and we had to ask the administration to stop bringing the army to watch the gate.

But to me, all these events were indeed good for my build up. I grew up into the young man that I am today, that I am proud of, because I never had any favour before me. Everything was a hustle, nothing appeared to me on a silver platter.

In most times, I found myself appearing in dreams in the most amazing places, sometimes in the most horrible places, doing the things I always did while back there. I would scream in the nightmares, I fought all sorts of wars in my sleep, winning some and getting killed in a few. I would mimic sounds of all types of guns each time I went to bed. Well, I don't know if that's true, but the people I slept with said so.

I killed because if I didn't, they would kill me.

I have to admit that my journey has been full of surprises. I regret many, but the truth is that I have a different take on life, one that was not like that which my family offered. Those surprises, I wouldn't expect them coming.

Then when I got home, I never slept in the house within the first month, I slept in the bush, alone.

I was too afraid, but desperate to live.

The same things continued haunting me when I went back to boarding school. Whenever it was holiday, I didn't want to come back home. I had to talk to the school management to let me stay at school. They agreed and, to return the favour, I used to maintain the flowers on the school compound. The school had a prayer garden, where there was lady who used to look after the garden. That's where I ate food during the holidays and I survived.

Whenever I travelled home for holidays, I felt like I was heading into a lion's den. I used to have an IPod to obstruct me from my memories and thoughts.

I can say that, up to date, I have never had a peaceful sleep. I keep jumping in my sleep. I don't know why because I don't remember.

All I care about is that life is the greatest gift.

Starting to talk

I was too afraid to re-open a wound I have spent so many years trying to nurse, but then the horrible feeling and guilt were ripping me apart from the inside.

I started to tell my story to just one person. She showed me that she was ready to listen when I showed her the scars on my back, legs and feet.

I started to talk. She never gave up however much I could see it in her face how difficult it was to digest what I was saying

For two hours, I started to tell my story for the first time. Slowly by slowly, each time telling more and more.

A year ago, she asked if I could tell my story to a small audience. To me, she was asking for too much, but then when I realized that my audience was school children whose parents have been displaced by the same war, I saw the need. It wasn't simple.

At first I was scared, I was shaking, sweating and wanting to run away from the room.

The children listened in disbelief. Some of them were terrified. Afterwards some of them tried not to get close to me.

The encounter lifted a heavy load from my chest. From that day, I wanted to talk more

In time, I talked to various audiences. The way they reacted, absorbed my story, amidst sobs, gave me the courage to write this book.

The nefariousness of the LRA is impossible to perceive.

This has to drive us to set obligatory, worldwide recognized standards on human rights to ensure that they are not violated any more, especially amongst children.

I have relived my abduction and written every word of this story myself.

Alex Olango 2016

Chapter 1: Village childhood

I was born in 1990 in a village north of the River Nile, in the savannah area of northern Uganda. I was the third-born in a family of seven children, although only three of my siblings were of both my father and mother.

We lived in a typical African homestead, consisting of several grass-thatched mud huts that catered for our extended family. All the children slept in one hut. One would only be entitled to sleep alone after you built your own hut.

Besides my parents and siblings, the compound accommodated my grandmother as well as my aunt, two of my uncles and their families. All in all, we were over 20 people living in the homestead.

Everything was shared. The adults took turns cooking for the entire family. We, the children, would play and eat together in one big circle around a common *log mot* (literally to mean; 'wash your hand slowly, food is enough'). It's a very wide bowl.

Our homestead was 9 kilometres from the nearest health centre. But the clinic was only a place of last resort. Babies were delivered by traditional midwives, at home. Illnesses, from malaria to diarrhoea, were treated with herbs. When somebody had a stomach upset, the person was given roots of a mango tree, pounded and mixed with water, to drink. When somebody had a wound, it was covered with leaves of black jack shrub. And when somebody had a fracture, the 'bone setter' would make a cast from pounded leaves and wrap it around the broken limb. Sometimes grandmother would call a witchdoctor, who performed a ceremony to expel the evil spirits. If everything else failed, the patient would be taken to the health centre on the back of a bicycle.

I was a happy playful boy. We would swim in the river, play soccer with a ball made of banana fibre, play hide and seek, rope skipping, *"cupu lawala"* and bird hunting expeditions using catapults.

We would also hunt wild animals, such as antelopes, warthogs and or *anyiri* (edible rats), using spears, clubs, bow and arrows, all with the help of our hunting dogs. On our way back, every child carried a log of wood on the shoulder for the evening fireplace. Those evenings were something every child looked forward to. The fireplace was an informal school where we learnt a lot about our cultural norms, our history and traditions. My favourite time of the day was sunset, when we would squat around the fireplace and listen to stories. My grandmother, in particular, was a great storyteller. She would teach us about Acholi culture and things that happened in the village. She would also tell us how she met her husband, and about the heroic hunting expeditions she took part in.

From my grandmother, I learned about the wars that had engulfed our country since independence. I learned about Idi Amin, the brutal dictator who overthrew the government of Milton Obote in 1971 and killed very many Acholi in the army. My grandfather, who had been a soldier in Obote's army, was forced to flee Amin's onslaught. Grandmother also told us about the Karamojong cattle rustlers, whom she hated even more than Amin's soldiers. The Karamojong took advantage of the chaos that followed the 1986 coup by Yoweri Museveni, to invade Acholiland and raid all the cattle.

"That is how the Acholi region became poverty-stricken," my grandmother said. "Cows were our wealth."

In one raid, my father, had his 30 cows stolen and was left with only two bulls. Father had cut off the legs of the bulls, so that they would not be taken. He hid from the Karamojong and, when they had gone, he came back to kill the bulls and smoke the meat to preserve it.

Like many Acholi, she blamed Museveni, accusing his government of having distributed guns to the Karamojong.

From the stories around the fire, I also learned about Alice Lakwena, the mysterious Acholi woman who claimed the Holy Spirit had instructed her to overthrow Museveni's government.

Grandmother said people willingly joined Lakwena's movement and mobilised food for her soldiers. They believed she would protect the Acholi against massacres, such as those committed by Idi Amin. Maybe, one day, their cattle would be returned.

But the stories that affected me most, filling me with fear and horror, were those about Joseph Kony. After Lakwena's forces were defeated, this Acholi 'son of the land' had gathered the remnants of her army and continued her mission to overthrow the government. However, his Lord's Resistance Army (LRA) had started abducting children and forcibly recruiting them into his army.

My father was the local councillor of the village & had worked for about 6 years. In 1987, when Kony said all local councillors were government spies and should be killed, my father had no choice but to join Museveni's army. As a toddler, I did not see much of him. My father was not as black as many Acholi people, but brown, tall, broad shouldered and bald. He would come home once or twice a year, each time for about two weeks. But I knew he loved my siblings and me very much. Every time he came home, he would bring each one of us something – a tin of beef or biscuits.

I was still very young when my father was killed. We were told that one morning, his commander entered his hut at the barracks to wake him up and he shot at his commander, wounding him in the arm. The commander then shot him dead. We have never been able to verify this story. Maybe my father thought it was the LRA. Or maybe the story was made up. Fear prevented us from finding out what happened. We had no transport or communication means at the time and we did not know whom to ask.

My father was killed just after my younger brother was born so my mother was left to care for four children. She is a chocolate brown-skinned, medium height, humorous, hardworking, strong woman. Every morning she and the elder kids went to the garden to cultivate food crops – sorghum, simsim (sesame) and cassava. I also went with them to the garden, babysitting our youngest. She collected firewood, and fetched water that she carried in a jerry-can on her head on her way back from the garden everyday. As is the custom among the Acholi, my late father's brother inherited my mother as a wife. He was and is supposed to take care of the family and continue producing children with her. That is how my only sister, Apio was born.

Meanwhile, the LRA war was coming closer and closer, surrounding us like dark clouds on the horizon. One day, in late 1996, people came running from other villages, screaming: 'The rebels are coming'. We ran away. All of us took refuge in the house of the local councillor. We stayed there the entire day but nothing happened. We returned home in the evening. A few days later, another rumour spread and we fled again. The story repeated itself three times but nothing happened. The rebels never showed up. The fourth time we ran to the home of the local councillor, the rebels stormed his house. It was my first time to be face to face with soldiers of the Lord's Resistance Army. There were about 20 of them. I was only five but I remember thinking that they looked smart in their army uniforms, which was quite confusing and deceiving. We all used to know that the rebels never had proper clothing. This was a disguise; they didn't want the local people to recognise them. At first we thought they were government army, only that the hairstyle was different. The LRA had dreadlocks and they spoke our language, contrary to the Swahili spoken by the government army.

    The rebels abducted six boys from among our group that had taken refuge in the local councillor's compound. I was considered too small. My elder brother was not taken either, because he had guinea worm and could not walk.

The LRA commander addressed us. He said that he did not want people to run away from them, that they were not bad people and they needed our support.

"We are fighting for our people. These children will fight for you and then come back," he told us.

Everybody was fearful. Parents pleaded with the commander not to take their children.

"My child is sick. Please, leave him," some said. But the commander said they had doctors and medicines in the bush; they would be fine. The rebels then looted the homestead and ordered three adults to carry the loot.

We were so traumatised that we remained in the local councillor's house for several days. One evening, our uncle went to check out our homestead and found that the rebels had not reached there, and so we returned home. We stayed home for some days and nothing happened. Then reports reached us from other villages that more children were being abducted. The adults who had been forced to carry the loot returned and reported that the LRA was mistreating the abducted children. They said they were tied with ropes, beaten and those who tried to escape were killed.

So in November 1998, at the age of 8, I was re-born into the insurgency when the war with the Lord's Resistance Army started to claim a lot of its own Acholi people. After that, I knew no peace at all. All I learned in childhood was to survive, no matter what.

"If you want to protect your children, leave for the camps," people said. The government had started opening Internally Displaced People's camps, saying it was unable to protect people in their villages, since the number of soldiers was too few.

We left for one of the IDP camps in northern Uganda. My mother carried my little sister. I carried clothes and blankets while my brother carried maize and cooking utensils. My stepfather did not want to leave the village yet and stayed behind with his other family. When we reached the camp, we found several hundred people already there. I had never seen so many people. From a homestead of about 20 people, I suddenly found myself in a place with over 800 people. It was like a small town. The hygiene was horrific. We built our own '*bolo*', a small hut made of reed and grasses.

At the beginning, in some ways, the camp was better than home. The army was around and we felt safe. There were many children my age so I had many friends. The government was encouraging more people to move to the camps. When some people refused to corporate, a couple of curfews were implemented. This involved beating up people, setting ablaze homesteads that were uncooperative and even killing stubborn heads of families.

As the IDP population increased, non-government organisations (NGOs), like Red Cross, Medecins Sans Frontieres, Save The Children, UNICEF, World Vision, World Food Programme and many more, came in. They distributed food, blankets and jerry-cans. They also installed mobile latrines, water tanks and piped water. Relatives who lived near the camp gave us two acres of land and we hired an additional two acres. My brothers and I helped my mother to cultivate food. Apart from the usual cassava and sorghum, we also grew beans and ground nuts.

There was a school in the IDP camp, so I started attending the school. We studied under trees. Since there were no chairs or desks, we were sitting on the ground and since there were no books or pens, we would write in the sand. The teachers would mark our work right there in the sand. The school population increased rapidly. Schools in surrounding villages relocated to the camp. The foster school was soon accommodating the pupils of three IDP schools. A feeding programme was set up at school, which attracted even more pupils, which was inevitable. We barely had enough to eat at home; therefore school was the best option to suit the situation. AVSI, an international NGO, built temporary structures. However, the classrooms were extremely crowded. There were more than 100 children in my class. Despite the poor learning environment, I loved school.

To earn some additional income, my mother washed the soldiers' clothes. That is how she met my second stepfather, who was an army man. He moved in with us not long after we joined the camp. However, he had five children with two other wives who had initially left him with all five children. He was actually looking for a woman to cater for the children. That woman he found in my mother. My mother, who was the third wife, ended up looking after his five children and producing another two with him. Soldiers in the army were not paid highly. Moreover, most of my stepfather's salary went to his first two wives' children. He never paid any school fees for any of us. But my mother never complained. To her, the security found in this man's company was more than enough.

As the years passed, the population in the camp rose to unsustainable levels. By 2001, the number of displaced people had shot up from 800 to 3,000. The army seemed no longer able to protect the camps. They themselves started to steal from our farms because their salaries were sometimes paid so late or even not at all for months.

"We can't sleep hungry when there is a gun in our hands" was a phrase used by Idi Amin when his soldiers complained about not being paid well.

Every night the rebels would sneak in. First it was common theft, then the army that was supposed to be guarding the camp started to break into small shops, rape the girls and the women and abduct children. Fire started to break out. All the little things we had were burned with our house. Hundreds of people were roasted alive in their own huts across northern Uganda in the insurgency. Again, we lived in a temporary structure, raised at the height of a camping tent, with reeds and grass as the only building material for construction.

The bush was a safer place to spend sleepless nights than in grass thatch huts. The rebels constantly crept into the camp and set grass roofs ablaze. If it wasn't your lucky day, you could easily become one of them

At the first sign of darkness each evening, we headed into the bush, but it rained on us most nights and we would stand under he trees to shelter from the tropical rain. Because it was the rainy season, the rebels had run out of foodstuffs, giving them a reason to constantly attack the IDP camp. They showed up any time of day or night. It didn't matter to them when they attacked. Not a single day did I sleep with both eyes closed. Sleep was impossible most nights because sounds made by crickets were replaced with sounds of bullets and military vehicles. Death was hovering all over the IDP camp. We were afraid of our own breath. It wasn't possible to believe in tomorrow. It practically didn't exist.

We barely had enough to eat. Sometimes my mother would surrender her share because there was never enough and, once in a while, we both surrendered our shares to the kids.

One day we were at school. It was about 2 p.m. when there were gunshots everywhere. The teachers managed to keep all the pupils inside the class until the shots were gone. School was closed and we were sent home. As we left school, we bumped into soldiers guarding the IDP camp, singing a war victory song.

Nyeko Talbert had reached his expiry date. He was a very influential man, a lieutenant in the LRA. His name was all over the region for the role he played. He used to cut off ears lips, noses or even plucked out the eyes of abductees who didn't follow his words.

Both hands bound to a rope anchored to the back of a military jeep, they were dragging the corpse of Talbert, a fallen LRA hero. The soldiers were lifting high their comrade who shot Talbert and the civilians joined in the celebrations. The soldiers parked the jeep in the middle of the trading centre, stripped the corpse naked, the army uniform and gumboots given to the shooter as a reward for the good job he had done. Then, in turn, the soldiers kicked, slapped and punched the corpse before they called the civilians to have fun with Talbert.

'This man raped your daughters, cut off the ears of those you love. Come and make him pay for these.' yelled the commander.

I had never seen an angry mob before. They practically ripped this man of his skin in minutes. The soldiers then went ahead and made a shallow grave for his remains in the barracks. Talbert was finally buried in a kneeling position.

As the insecurity mounted and the number of people in the camps increased day by day, the NGOs left one after the other and the food rations were no longer sufficient. Things changed so fast that it wasn't safe any more. With everything falling apart at the IDP camp, my mother decided to send me to my aunt in Gulu to pursue my primary studies.

"It's safer in town." she reassured me.

"But I don't even know their homes" I said.

I didn't stay at home for another week. At the age of 11, I bade my mother farewell and climbed onto a pick-up truck headed for the big town, every passenger looking more terrified of the trip than the other.

The trip was longer than anticipated. Normally it took one hour, but this time we took four solid hours on the same road. There was a roadblock ahead of the pick up truck. When we got to the site, we saw there had been a land mine. A man was blown into pieces. He was meat – fresh. The left foot was hanging in a thicket by the roadside. Only the clothes identified him. I barely had anything in my stomach the night before, but I managed to throw up my intestines.

Now we were back on the road, so bumpy and dusty. The pick up truck made too much noise. This scared the hell out of me. No, not me alone. Other faces flashed more fear than mine, even the driver. I could see he was shaking at the wheel. Another roadblock and the pick up truck halted. Everyone jumped out in a straight line. They were talking to us. My eyes were perfect and I did what others were doing. First, we took off our shirts. Women did too. Those with serious scars were weeded out. I got lucky. At eleven years of age my skin was perfect, rather more than perfect, like baby's skin. If someone had scars on his shoulders, it was a sign of carrying a gun. The army would hold you back to explain your scars. That day, the army took four people who had the scars they were looking for. God knows what happened to them.

After 30 minutes, another roadblock. Shirts off, checked for battle scars. We were handed slashers. Of course, they weren't proper slashers – they were tree branches. We had to slash the roadside, cutting down grass using tree branches. Hands blistered. There was no one to maintain the roads, therefore the travellers had to do it. The defence army was scared to do it. They wouldn't be caught unawares by the rebels.

I made it to Gulu town and, living with an aunt on the outskirts of town, life seemed better.

Once in the town, I was enrolled in Ongai Primary School, one of the many IDP schools that were relocated from Amuru district to Gulu town, for the safety of the children. Gulu Public Primary School gave us a couple of unfinished classrooms for the pupils in upper classes while the kids from the lower section took their classes under a few trees.

They served lunch at school. I loved it. As I grew familiar with the school, I realised one thing. Children from the host school often mocked us, calling us all sorts of names. There was too much stigma. I didn't want to study any more and I would cut classes.

At weekends when we were off school, my aunt baked some cakes that I carried on my head to sell in town, sometimes I would carry sugar canes on my shoulder to sell. The money was to support the family

My aunt and her five children lived in Limo, a 30-minute walk from school. But this suburb was not as safe as we thought. The rebels were all around the town, striking the suburbs and nearby villages at night looting and abducting children.

I was already an old man in a young boy's skin.

Chapter 2: Night commuting

I ended up joining the tens of thousands of child 'night commuters' in Gulu town, sleeping in many of the improvised night shelters, for fear of being abducted.

Every day, I rushed home after school for the evening meal and walked back to town at sunset. Together with my aunt's kids, we would select a place to sleep on one of the crowded pavements, in the bus park or at the rice milling factory and spread out our sacks that served as mattresses. At sunrise, we got up, walked home to wash our faces and legs, dusty with running, and rushed to school.

Night commuting was worse than sleeping in the bush. I lost so many blankets that my aunt refused to buy any more. I never intended to lose one. You woke up in the middle of the night and it was gone. Someone needed it more than I did, I guess. The whole situation was pretty much confusing. The army on patrol would gather all the girls who were commuting. They would convince them of a 'safe' place, which never existed. They were all raped and threatened to keep quiet about it or else, at the point of guns. Who would dare talk? Most girls were raped. This was in the middle of Gulu town, but there were lots of thieves and child molesters at the night shelters.

During rainy nights, people would also fight for the few dry places. One day it had rained. The verandas were a little bit dry. I marked my place with charcoal. While I was still trying to lay my mat, a man, way older than me, stopped me. He was smoking.

"I booked that corner." he said.

"No. I got there first." I replied.

I went ahead and set out my mat and called my aunt's boys, who I commuted with, into bed. The man sprung up from whatever he was smoking, grabbed our mat and threw it into the rain. He laid his mat in my place. I was angry. I wanted to fight. Adrenalin couldn't form. I was too afraid. No, I told myself, swung to the guy, grabbed his mat and threw it into the rain. His hands were so wide and so big. His open hand covered three quarters of my face. I found myself struggling to get out of a trench. He was back, smoking his God knows what, lying comfortably in my place.

I took the kids to the next street. My aunt's kids were younger than me. They were my responsibility each night. We found a dry veranda and laid to rest, but my anger was eating me from inside. It was pay back time. I waited until the kids fell asleep. I found a broken bucket. In it, I put water from the drain, my own urine and some food remains from a rubbish heap. It was a nuclear bomb, perfect smell for the use. I walked to this man. He was snoring in the comfort of my own place. Yes, I had booked it for the kids and me. It was my place. I emptied the contents of the bucket. His clothes, bedding and himself were soaked in sewage. I was gone into the darkness, a battle won.

I stayed in Gulu for only a few months. I did not like the way other pupils in the school treated us. They used to call us all sorts of names; like sons of rebels, villagers, street kids, vultures and many others. They even called us rebels. So after one term, I decided to return to the camp. All those months I was away, I never stopped thinking of Mummy, how she was coping without my help, because I was her anchor, on many occasions.

While I kill,
I cannot judge,
I cannot hate and
I cannot separate myself from life.
I can only be joyful because I am still
alive and whole.
This is why I kill.

Chapter 3: Abduction

Footsteps from the riverbank. An armed man appears. He was wearing a black gumboot on his right leg, a green one on the left leg, both gumboots made of "kiraga", patches from mending torn pieces of rubber stuck together with heated knives, an army jacket and a pair of pants fully torn apart. I couldn't tell the colour or when they were last washed. The man had long dreadlocks. I couldn't make out the face. That was all covered in the dreadlocks. Even from a distance, I could observe the creamy-white eggs of lice from his hanging hair.

There was nothing to hesitate about. I was standing face to face with a Lakwena. That's how we, the Acholi people, call rebels.

'Don't run.' the man murmured while reaching out for his gun.

I could see how rusty the end of the barrel was. He had two magazines, one appended to the other on the gun by rubber bands. I have no idea whether the guns were loaded. They could even be empty. But a gun will always look ugly.

I jumped out of the water to the other side of the river and helped out my two siblings from the water. We started to run, but the kids couldn't manage my pace. I stopped.

'Run, run.' I begged them to get away.

They were too young to be taken. That was all I could do to save them from this man. He didn't see which path the kids took, because he was busy trying to get across the river. I led him to a rough path, away from where the kids went. He was on my tail. This path hadn't been used for some time and the grasses were taller than me, bending over the path from both sides making a tunnel that led to a garden. I ran and tried to listen, I couldn't hear any footsteps after me. For a second, it was a relief, though I didn't stop or even think of it. My breath was heavier than my weight. I was panting like a pig.

I don't know how, but Opoka, the rebel chasing me, was waiting right ahead, at the garden where the path led. He threw a piece of firewood at me and it tangled round both my legs. I went to the ground with a thunderous fall. I tried to get back to my feet, my nerves refused to respond. I went to the ground again. This time, he hit me right on the head, with the butt of his gun. The pain ran right through the head to the feet. I pretended I was dead, thinking he would have mercy and leave me behind.

He was breathing so heavily, right over my head.

'Get up.' he shouted.

I could tell from the way he sounded, that this man was madly angry with me. I was trying so hard not to breathe. I wanted him to believe that I was dead. I could hear him try to get his breath back to normal. He was coughing really badly. While at school, I used to run 3000 metre races. I am sure I gave him a little taste of who I was.

He reached out to his gun, put it right at the back of my head. Now I wanted to "resurrect" from my faked death.

'Please don't shoot', I cried in my heart, not wanting him to hear.

All I wanted was for this merciless man to ask me to get up. He didn't. Instead, he opened the safe of his weapon. For a moment, I thought I was dead. No, he didn't shoot me. My fingers could move. I freaked out. He was not talking now, only doing. Opoka cocked his weapon. I started to sweat.

Opoka was not joking. 'You want him to do something else again?' I asked myself. I knew the answer to the question. I don't need to answer my own questions, just do what Opoka does - no talking. I sprung up.

'Please don't shoot.' I cried. This time, it was a loud cry for mercy.

'On your knees.' he barked, as if I was deaf. He hit me again, on the shoulder with the butt of his AK47. I swear I was almost on my knees before he even barked. Both hands bound to the back, he kicked, slapped and whipped me all over till we got to the rest, who were across the river because I tried to get away from them. I saw four friends of mine. They too were victims. I could see how terrified they were, but I was more terrified. I was the youngest.

Our home was across this river. I led them home, as they demanded. My cousin, a few months younger than me, was pounding roasted simsim (sesame) for dinner. She was alone at home. She tried to run, two men went after her. They didn't take long before grabbing her. I never wanted to shed tears. I couldn't bear the fact that we both might not ever return to our people and the huge responsibility, to watch over her while out there. How was I supposed to do this?   I had to cry, because I didn't know what to do.

Huts and granaries were set ablaze. The rebels took whatever they thought was necessary and set the rest into flames.

The "Kadogos", the young soldiers, were heartless and they were dancing round the flames, blowing whistles and singing victory songs. They became this way because some of them saw their family members locked in the huts and roasted while they were taken. The same thing could have happened to mine, had they found my mother and the kids at home. The rebels did this so that the abducted boys had nowhere and no one to return to.

'Your only home is the bush.'

They often reminded us of our homelessness without them. As a kid, I gave up on so many things in life that day.

They made us victims so they would 'rescue' us, yet the truth is, they preyed on our pain. Relentless manipulation, how would we know? I didn't want it to be true but I could feel it was. One wonders why some of us never became lifelong liabilities to the movement. Well, because we were tired of being lied to.

'Please let me get my shirt on', I cried

'Shut up and follow the route', one man shouted, pointing to the path leading to nobody knew where.

Twenty juveniles were taken, bound together with a single rope round the waists. In this way, escaping was not possible.

Gunpowder smells terrible, becoming worse with fresh blood and spiced with loud cries for help. I knew the worst had come when the government army came after us. They tried in vain to rescue us, innocent children. No stopping, no talking; only running all night. The only means of communication were whips on the back and sharp insults about our parents. I was strong. I had got used to living without my Dad, since he didn't wait for me to get to know him that much. He died too soon. I don't even remember crying at his funeral. That is how young I was, though I knew he loved me so much.

That night, I remained bare-chested, no food in the stomach but I was not hungry. With a panga in my hand, I had cut shrubs ahead of us to make the way through the thick bush. Dew showered me from head to toe but the fear in me was too great to let me complain. We moved through "Gang romo" literally meaning village of the sheep. It was a village that had been abandoned, but sheep left behind. Lakwena rebels rejoiced whenever they got to this place, because meat was in abundance. Night was peaceful. I caught some sleep but kept waking up before I could close both eyes. People roasted meat overnight, while others visited the bush every minute because almost everyone had diarrhoea that night.

At around 1 a.m., it was time for entertainment. We were made to fight one another. The one who made the other one bleed first was ranked higher than the other until the strongest was found. I remember that day I fought with four boys and was victorious. Almost all soldiers gained interest in me. They all wanted me as an escort. This made life even more complicated for me in the first few days as a boy soldier.

When we reached evening, this group selected 18 soldiers, giving each a matchbox. They had the mission to go to burn down the IDP (Internally Displaced People) camp of mud & thatch huts, in my own village. I grew up in this camp.

The darkest moment of my life happened the following morning, the morning following our abduction. As soon as our parade was dismissed, Lapwony Tabule, the commander, called everyone in front of his tent.

One of the new recruits, probably abducted the day before, tried to escape that second evening. It wasn't a lucky day for him. This boy, about 10 years of age, was abducted from a trading centre about 30 kilometres away from my own village. They brought him back to the camp and bound both hands and legs to a tree.

'I want all of us to know that escaping is unforgivable. He will help to show us what happens when one tries to escape.' Lapwony Tabule angrily uttered these words. After a long silence, he lifted his head and told his escort to slice the young boy's throat. They collected the blood in a saucepan as we watched. As though that wasn't enough, he busted the skull open and emptied the brain into the blood collected. With a mingling stick, the two boys stirred the mixture into a 'porridge'. That spectacle was a warm-up.

Lapwony Tabule walked up to the boys who made 'porridge' of blood and brains. Quietly, he dipped his two fingers into the 'porridge' and licked it. He did this three times. We were arranged into single file. In turn, we fed on the 'porridge', the boys licking three times, the girls four. It was part of our LRA culture.

I felt so empty, as if my soul had suddenly left my body. There was numbness all over my body, a shower of sweat soaked my hands and heels. One of the abducted girls refused to feed off their mixture. With a vegetable knife, they got to her throat and her blood was added to the 'porridge'.

That night was the quickest night I have ever known. Fear completely took control. It wasn't possible to be me again. The trick worked magic on me. I was one of them.

Chapter 4: Crossing the river

A gunshot. "Everybody, grab your luggage." yelled the commander as he led the group into the woods.

The LRA groups often left 3 to 5 soldiers a kilometre away from a new campsite. They were referred to as 'guards'. The guards lay an ambush a kilometre away on the entry to the new campsite. They were meant to keep away any intruders into the campsite and the group in the camp always took off upon hearing a gunshot from the guards. The first gunshot served as a warning. The LRA had another individual called an 'Op'. He was supposed to climb into a tree. His elevation helped keep watch for intruders from a distance, especially those who didn't follow the same route that the group used to get into the camp, meaning the guards would miss out on spotting this threat. But the "Op" kept the group safe by firing a shot into the air when he saw a threat and the group deserted the camp.

The guards caught up with the group at sunset, the army on our tails.

A day and a half without food or water, but the greater fear kept me going. I didn't want to risk escape but I didn't want to be a rebel.

When we finally got to a sub-county of Gulu District, we had to cross a river.

The rebels used the recruits, especially the old ones, as though they weren't human beings. You can't just send a man into a roaring river to see its strength. Young recruits are sometimes pardoned. When the old ones mess up, you are gone; they slice your throat like a pineapple.

'Another person', shouted the commander.

All were trying to make it to the back of the line to avoid being picked, the blood hungry *kadogos* are heading towards us. To them, this was cinema. Who would want to enter that water? We all saw what it did to the first two victims. The water took both feet of the first man, the moment he stepped in, and his head hit a rock. The second man, everyone thought he would make it to the other side, but a crocodile was waiting for him almost at the other shore. The crocodile took him, a thick line of blood ran down the river as the man screamed for help. And now they were looking for the third man standing to be thrown to the lion's den.

'You, come here', a *kadogo* shouted, pointing to one young man.

He was probably 6 years older than me from his physical looks. This man refused to come out of the line. He hit him with the butt of his gun

"Please I can't swim", the man begged.

"Who do you want to see die?" asked one of the *kadogos.*

'Get yourself up and cross the river with this rope.'

'Do you want your people to see you again?'

The man stopped crying; he grabbed the rope and without looking at anyone jumped into the water. This man was just afraid. He could swim better than the other two who didn't make it.

I could see how he fought the current. One big wave swallowed him up and I thought that was the end. The thought of losing three people at one spot was eating me up but the thought of being the next victim made it even worse.

"Back to the line" shouted the commander as we toppled each other to get to the line.

I could see he was as angry as I was, but at whom? I had no idea. This man is planting all the orders, now it's our fault we can't swim. Well, me I could swim, but have never seen such enormous water my whole life, the water that can tear down its own banks, the one which can split a log of wood like an axe.

"He made it", one recruit shouted.

We all dashed to the scene. He was there, hanging onto a straw, shivering and panting so heavily. I could see from a distance, he was terrified. There was blood coming from his head, he bruised the head on a rock probably.

"Don't try anything stupid or we shall shoot you", said the commander.

He thought the man would chose to run away since he is now on the other side of the river. Three men pointed their weapons at him as he tried to get to a nearby tree.

He found a tree and tied the rope onto it. We also tied the other end to a big tree to make a hang line just above the water level.

One soldier went first, his gun strapped tightly to his back. He then grabbed the rope with both hands. The legs and stomach all inside the water, following the hang line, he made it to the other side of the river. Then we started to cross, just the way he did, one person at a time.

Many of us lost our luggage to the water. I was carrying a 20 kilogram bag of beans and had to strap it to my back like a baby. While I reached almost the middle of the water, the water current became too strong. It pulled my left hand off the rope. I knew it was the bag bringing me the problem. With one hand, I quickly untied the bag from my back. The water took it and I became a bit lighter. With all the remaining energy, I forced my left hand back to grab the rope. I did it and this time I made sure it never came off again until I got to the other side.

Even with the rope, you could see people being taken. The water was too much. I thought I would never swim again. It was horrible. Even if you didn't know those people who didn't make it across, people are people, just like you. It kills you from the inside if you see someone brutally dying, especially those crying for your help and you can't do anything about it.

It took me time to get over this or have I ever got over this scene in the bush?

This covered most parts of my dreams when I returned home a long time later. I would have nightmares. This time it was either my mother or siblings being taken by water. Sometimes I got drowned in my own dreams.

My two friends didn't make it. I am not sure; did they get shot or escape? This made it even worse for me. I was given fifteen canes the following morning for not keeping an eye on those two. They even assigned a soldier to keep an eye on me. They didn't trust me a single bit.

This camp was within a tributary, where two rivers join. It was safe because the army had to fight the river before getting to the camp and, in case this happens, the river is the most strategic place to lay an ambush. That's why the army didn't pursue us; they would have lost a crowd.

Soon we ran out of foodstuff. We fed on boiled sorghum for days. A group was sent to the trading centre to get food that evening. It rained heavily and the river was full, so the group didn't make it back to the campsite until morning. The army followed them and took back the supplies they had looted. They all returned but barely alive. Our little hideout was no longer safe and hunger weakened even the bravest hearts I used to know. I personally ate a complete tube of toothpaste – yes, it did tell my tummy a little. Hunger kills, I can testify to that. Sorghum soup was my favourite for almost a week. There was no salt but it was perfect for the situation. The result was that soon we all had ballooned cheeks.

To make things worse, our commander always had smoked meat to eat. The aroma was all we got, even if you were picked to prepare the meal. They could break the bones from smoked meat in your face. Then you had to wash the dishes – even the sight of bones made my stomach grumble.

God wasn't the best of friends with me.
I hated God because He couldn't keep me away from the rebels.
God didn't protect me.
God didn't matter.

It was just me, alone against the world.

I missed home.

When we went to the river, we would swim, spit, urinate, defecate in the water before filling the jerry-cans with drinking water and yet no-one fell sick, Amazing!

I stood under the tree. Last light of the day was leaving us, though as soon as the rain came, it ruined our plan.

Chapter 5: Opoka

Opoka walked to me. He was taken into the bush a year before me. Opoka was now a trusted soldier. I was surprised to see him. I remember dancing and eating at his funeral. He was presumed dead and the parents made a huge funeral service. His father had money; he had a big shop. I remember a child was once asked in Primary 2 what he wanted to be when he grew up.

"I want to be Opoka's father" he answered with great anxiety.

The whole class clapped for him. He was right, me too.

When he was abducted, no-one knew his real name. He lied and that is how he got his new identity – Opoka.

Opoka was changed. He was a true rebel. They could send him to his own village for an operation. He would not try to escape.

"It's almost dark, isn't it?" he asked.

I tried to talk but everyone could see it was almost dark, so I just looked at him.

"Don't be afraid." he said.

Still I had no word for him. Despite the assurance, I was getting afraid. His presence didn't mean well to anybody. That's what other recruits said of him too. He was a chameleon.

Kony had called for a retreat. Everyone under command was to report for South Sudan.

The same feeling I had a year ago flooded me.

We were in Gulu District. Opoka never stopped. He always wanted to be friends. My list was full, of course with no friends. It's me against the world. This sentence kept me going for some time. It was safer this way because no one knew what you felt or what you thought.

"You know, I could help." Opoka whispered.

"What are you talking about?" I asked.

"Do you want to be like me?" he asked me.

I didn't say a thing. This guy knows it's wrong. He gave me the look.

"This is no life, my friend." I could read it all over his face.

That evening, I walked up to his tent. Opoka had a simple tent. That is what you are rewarded with for a good job done in the LRA setting, the luxury of sleeping under a tent. He quickly signalled me inside, looked out so make sure no one was close enough to eavesdrop on our conversation. Then he came back inside the tent. Opoka reminded me of the danger if I chose to stay.

"Remember your mother is waiting." he exclaimed.

Without thinking, I agreed with him.

"I want to escape." I said.

"I will help you, but don't let anyone know this."

Actually he forced this into my head by pulling both my ears.

"What did I just say?" he asked.

"Don't let anyone know this." I replied as he released my ears and walked away.

He left me in his tent.

I was trying hard to keep my cool. Opoka's place seemed a horrible place. Something told me to leave the tent. First he terrified me. It was all in my head. My mother was waiting. Trying so hard to believe him, I sat down on the floor of his hut. Then my heart missed a beat.

Something always warned me of danger. I sprang to my feet. It was too late. I could hear Opoka replaying our previous conversation, by his mouth, to someone. I had messed up real big. Opoka was replaying me to Lapwony Tabule. It is a matter of life and death. I should never have jumped into his lap, I told myself helplessly.

I was beaten. I stopped counting the lashes at the fifth, passed out, only to wake by the cold breeze of dawn, chained to a tree. Shorts off, with ants feeding from the wounds. I had no hands to chase away the ants from the wounds. Both hands and legs were tied up. The mosquitoes all had red abdomens. They really fed. I was sweating and shivering from cold at the same time.

Opoka got to me first. He flashed me with a wicked smile.

"How stupid can you be?" He whispered into my ear.

I hated him. He needn't remind me. I was more stupid than he thought. I sucked it in before it came out.

"Thank you for the treat." I spat this at him. He was quiet for about a minute.

'Look,
While I kill,
I cannot judge,
I cannot hate and
I cannot separate myself from life.
I can only be joyful because I am still alive and whole.
This is why I kill.
Get a life, stupid!'

He spat the horrible words into my face and walked away.

Then he turned around, as though he had left something behind. "Pray hard that they don't kill you" he whispered into my ear. This time, he walked away for real.

I noticed that there were streams of tears running down to my lips. I was crying without sound, so painful to cry from the inside. I didn't pray.

Despite being horrible, I always remember what he told me. "Mummy is waiting." This sentence made me smile each time. I thought about it. It often strengthened me whenever I was feeling low. I had a reason to return home one day, Mummy of the kids.

Chapter 6: Tinka

I was in ropes the whole day. No food or water, I wasn't hungry, thought I wouldn't need it any more. Then lots of virtual thoughts flashed right into my face.

I could see my Dad smiling back to me. He would say, "Be strong" and he was gone.

It was almost noon. The heat was too much. My nose started bleeding, hands tied to the back. There was nothing I could do to stop the bleeding. I always experienced this when it was too hot, my nose bled – and it still happens.

Tinka, another new recruit, dashed to report this. They did nothing. I was covered in my own blood. The bleeding stopped when there was no more blood flowing to the head, I suppose. I fainted. The pain in my buttock, I could feel the pricks. Another stab of pain through my back. Conscious again, this time I am not in the sun. Tinka was there; he was to keep watch. Tinka was two years older than me, such a kind boy. A little noisy though; he could easily betray. That was my feelings towards him. We never talked before, just because I didn't want to make friends. Tinka gave me water, half a cup. It wasn't enough but it didn't matter, it was all he had. The pain was unbearable. I could feel balls of hot tears racing down my cheeks. My soul was crying. How embarrassing to cry in front of your age mate.

"It's OK" said Tinka.

I tried to talk; couldn't. I didn't know what to say. Just tears. I was afraid.

"Thank you, Tinka." I said.

"I am going to tell them that you are awake." he said.

"No, no, no. Please don't." I cried.

"OK, will you be fine if I leave?" not wanting to hear my cries any more.

Now the ropes were being removed. Lapwony Tabule and Lapwony Okidi were standing there. This was no good. Tinka didn't return. Maybe they would tell me everything would be fine.

"You will live, you son of a slut." Okidi said.

"Lucky bastard", Lapwony Tabule interrupted.

I didn't know I hadn't finished my canes. I fainted too early. Now I was supposed to take the remaining 35 lashes. Seriously, there wasn't anywhere to beat any more. My butt was three times swollen more than normal. I couldn't even sit on it, now those people wanted to beat it. You were always given a choice to make. That was, chose what they want.

I lay down, stuffed my shirt in my mouth and gave them my butt. The first six were chilli hot, then the rest felt like they were beating a sponge. I remained awake this time A hundred canings. I had cleared my debt.

I spent three days nursing my wounds. No medicine, just hot water and salt. Sometimes alone, but Tinka was always there. He went to the river, boiled the water and stole the salt to put in the wounds. Tinka made me a walking stick. I was able to walk after a solid week.

Chapter 7: To Sudan

Other groups started to arrive. Our group was led by Lapwony Tabule. Then MAK4 group led by Odiambo and Stockree group led by Raska Lukwiya arrived last.

These three groups wanted to trek together, to Sudan. We had two weeks to make it to Sudan. I could hardly walk without a stick. This was the hardest walk. Not many new recruits made it. Their plan didn't go as planned. The army was too many. The retreat wasn't a success. We needed more soldiers, to make it to the border. They pushed us back. We camped where the place was safe. I became a Junior Soldier here. I had a gun. It wasn't mine but, all the same, this somehow made me feel safe and protected.

Lapwony Okidi adopted me to his household, his family. Sounds weird but the rebels had households, often a group of six with a head of that household. The members cooked together and ate together, just like a family. Lapwony Okidi had lost his escort when we attempted to get to the border into Sudan. His escort was crying for help, but everyone was running. Lapwony Okidi ran to him and took his gun, then turned to run. The boy was begging for help. He turned and shot him in the head.

"I was helping him", he said. "The army was going to kill him anyway", he added

Each day had something in store for me. I lost grip of my luggage while we fled from an army attack. In the backpack, there was an army uniform and a chain (full round) of bullets. Lapwony Okidi had killed an NRM army man in the series of fights. The uniform was almost new. Yes it was, but that doesn't change a thing. I hated it, because it was removed from a corpse. He still wanted me to wear it. Sometimes I didn't regret dropping my backpack. No, Acholi men are not good at lying. I did regret the loss. Not because of the uniform or bullets though. I had roasted cassava in one of the pockets. Now I had to go for days without something in the stomach. Now I had the feeling that this bag could be found and I wanted to race back before Okidi noticed. The problem was we were trekking non-stop. Let me accept the loss and the price of 15, 20 or 30 canes. I'm not sure I will walk again. I had first recovered but I thought there was something wrong with me.

Finally it was dark, everybody tired and scared. The NRM army gave up the chase. They were scared too. Darkness unfolds many things.

I wished he would carry me. Two days without food or water was way too much for me. I would sneak out and eat potato peelings. It was risky to let anyone see me eating anything. Then you would work for all members in that household.

At the end of my punishment, we had to find what to eat, but my punishment was extended by nature. I was going to die that third day, when we reached a deserted homestead. There were pawpaws on the trees. Hunger had gone to my brain. The world was spinning. I sat down to avoid a fall. My eyes were up in the trees. I wanted just one pawpaw. After gaining a little strength to pick it, I managed just one the size of my head. It worked, though the night was sleepless. However much I tried not to, I diarrhoeaed in my pants. I chose to live and that is what matters for now. I cleaned up next morning and, alive, we were heading east. I didn't know the places we were passing through but I knew our destination.

Our intelligence officer had tipped the group about a possible attack to the new camp, the following day. Very early the next morning, a jet plane passed over the camp. Smoke always betrayed the rebels. Any smoke gave the NRM army a clue. From experience, it never took the army more than three hours to launch an attack after a jet plane had passed over a rebel camp. That morning, we deserted the camp.

Now heading towards Lira District, I was afraid. My plan to escape was being brought to a halt. The Langi people, occupants of Lira and neighbouring districts, were naturally hostile, hating my Acholi tribe, because Joseph Kony, leader of the LRA rebels, is Acholi. The Langi people killed most individuals who tried to escape into their region. I knew what to do. Remain loyal. After hours, we entered Lira and humanity. I found recently dumped faeces on the roadside of the path. In some homesteads, we were welcomed with chicken, goats, sheep and pigs. The people were gone, though there were fresh footprints. Mixed feelings now, trying to be loyal but can't erase the possibility of being free again. The gun I was carrying had an empty magazine. I wouldn't be able to defend myself now. I didn't want to take the risk. It's the worst feeling when you don't know what to do. Us Acholi people are not used to conflicting situations, so we often went for the wrong choice.

I remembered my late uncle. The rebels killed him when I was eight years old. He was so traditional. I was living with his family one school holiday. That fateful day, his son and I had gone swimming. The stream was some distance away. The rebels got home before we returned. My uncle had received his retirement money, three million Uganda shillings and I was told that not many people could get that amount. He was a war veteran who fought in the Obote and Amin forces. Uncle had lost one eye before he was released from the forces. This money was partly resettlement and compensation.

He didn't know what to do with the money, so he secretly kept the money in the house. We didn't know banks then.

That day, the rebels were chatting with him. They were in his house and they wanted the money. Uncle chose not to give the money to them, even though they threatened to kill. That was the problem with being a soldier. Death threats never meant a thing. He was stabbed in the chest four times, with a bayonet. He never spoke. My cousin and his mother lost a great deal there. Uncle had not told them where the money was.

So, don't ask an Acholi to chose from two similar things, unless you are ready to go with the wrong one.

I was feeling sick. It wasn't a disease, just mad at the things I didn't know.

I blamed the Langi people for being hostile

I blamed and cursed the man who chased me and brought me into the bush, then the army.

I blamed God.

I remembered our small church, a big mango tree. A man dressed in white robes always told us that God makes all things possible, but today God was making things impossible.

I grabbed my gun and wanted to use it. The trigger went off. There was no sound, there was no bullet and I was still alive.

Then I thanked God for saving my life, before abusing Him again.

> I am sick because I can't escape.
> I am sick because my magazine is empty.
> I am sick because the people here are hostile.
> I am sick because I don't know what to do.

We camped at a homestead. There was cassava and I had a whole chicken to myself, roasted. There was no sleep. We had slaughtered four goats. These were to be ready to carry by sunrise. We stayed up all night, smoking the meat. I won't forget that day. I ate what could have been served to five men, alone.

I was loving the rebel life now I had meat. I wanted to stay, to eat more of this. It was strange to me. While at home, we had meat only at Christmas, even when the Acholi people still had cattle. Cattle were for status. The man with the largest herd of cattle was champion. My father didn't have that much. That made the whole thing complicated. He never killed his cattle for the family. The problem came when the Karamajong people raided the whole northern region. They took everything. Mother told us that Daddy cried for weeks. That didn't change a thing. The cattle were gone.

Rebel life was unpredictable. Today you were throwing food away, tomorrow you had barely anything to eat.

Things seemed perfect here in the village in Lira. It had been a week and the army seemed to give us some holiday. Some of us started gaining some weight, not the whole body of course. Our cheeks looked more healthy than the rest of the body; the moon face I learned in Science class.

Just as usual, that week was busy. The rebels called it Registration Week. They were training us to dismantle and reassemble the rifles and cleaning them. The real registration; I am about to be passed out. I am six months in the wilderness. That morning, eighteen recruits were almost crossing the line to be soldiers. The leader of one of the groups in the bush was invited to Lapwony Raska Lukwiya. He was tall and very dark. From the look, the blood that was running in his vessels was also black. This man was dangerous. He didn't smile. Now he was performing a ritual. He had shea nut oil and holy water. We were told that water was special. The container never went dry and it had never been refilled.

Raska made the sign of a cross on our foreheads and then put three drops of the holy water on our heads. The girls got four drops.

"With this, you are welcomed into this big family." he said. "This holy water will trace your whereabouts if any of you escape. The oil will make you return."

He said something like it makes you go mad and walk back to their arms.

This alone created all sorts of worries for me. I had wanted to be passed out, sent to look for foodstuff in the trading centre, so I would hide there. A simple escape plan.

But now what is the use? The holy water would trace my whereabouts and the oil would make me go back, for real and for good. I would rather stay here and remain normal.

The holy session was done.

Now we were assembled for physical registration. There were pangas, canes and a dog. They want the scars on the back not the butt.

The three weapons, panga, cane and dog were written on a piece of paper and folded. Now they were 'trying to be fair'. They wanted us to pick the weapon randomly. You picked what they would use to scar you. No one walks up to pick. Me too, I didn't. Now Raska threatened to use all three on each person. I jumped off the line, the folded papers so many. I wanted the cane. I closed my eyes and picked one. It's a panga. The pangas were first heated to almost brick red. I was about to faint, I sat down to breathe. Everyone picked.

There were sixty lashes, the whole back wounded. The flies want to carry me away. I couldn't put my shirt back on.

Two boys chose the dog. They tied up the dog on their back, like a mother carrying a baby. Then they beat the dog. The dog practically ate all the flesh on their backs. One of the boys lost his ear.

My panga turned out almost to be a better choice, if compared to what the dogs did to the two boys.

No treatment, only warm salted water was prescribed.

I stayed there three weeks, lying on my stomach when sleeping or resting. All the while, they had retrieved all the guns from us. I swear I would have shot someone.

The army was soon on our tail. The goats and chickens were no more. Hunger again. The good news was that I was wearing a shirt again now and the flies had given me a break. We had been walking bare footed all this while and my soles were as hard as a car tyre. I could put out fire with my heel.

We ran to the hills. The nature was perfect, the problem was that there was no food. The place was deserted way too early. No gardens and huts almost falling down. The hills kept us safe but the stomachs were lonely. The army guarding an IDP camp was tough. Several times, we tried to evade the camp, but they kept sending us back.

The group reorganised and we were heading north. Lapwony Madit, literally meaning The Boss, wanted his troops. I was told we were passing via my home district and didn't know any other place. I was born in my little village, raised there and destined to die there too. Travelling is not our thing in this country. Most people in Uganda are at one time tourists in their own home district.

This part of the country had a big problem, poverty. Many families, for example, mine, were poor to the level that we didn't know that we were poor. To tell you the truth, I got to know money when I was four years old. I still didn't know the value, just that it was money. I was almost five before I knew it had value. I started noticing that there were 50 shillings, 100 shillings.

I had always been a bright kid at school. I had to repeat P4, P5 and P6. I was first in all those three wasted years. My mother was worried, because I was going too fast through schooling. She was afraid I would finish up in P7 and need money for Secondary school. I repeated classes a lot to delay Secondary schooling. The painful moment when your friend returned home for holidays, they are three years ahead of you, just because you are broke and they are not. That is when I hated money.

We passed through my home area. There was always an eye on me because I could possibly escape. They called it walking. I refused. It was running. That was the pace.

Whenever I tried to walk, the gap remained. I had to run to keep up. All day running to catch up with the men, with sometimes a couple of whips, the pace was too much with a bag of beans on my back.

Darkness was swallowing the earth. I was thinking of resting, but we were walking all night. The goal was to get to the border before the light (a journey which was supposed to be covered in three days). They gave us thirty minutes to rest. I put down my bag of beans and sat on it. Thirty minutes was like thirty seconds. The whistle went off. We were on the track, only five kilometres away from Sudan.

Chapter 8: JuJu

Sometimes a lot of things happen within me and I can't explain. We had just walked about a kilometre ahead.

Something strange happened. Suddenly it was darker than the night in front of me. When I looked behind, it was as if it was daytime. There was darkness in front and day light behind. Then a cloud of fear covered me up, my heart raced fast. The heart racing wasn't a new thing to me. It often happened when I got myself into trouble. I decided to tell Lapwony Okidi. Okidi laughed it out. The vision didn't go. Whenever I looked behind, I saw the light. I told Okidi again. This time he lent me a good ear. He went to Lapwony Tabule, the leader of this group. Tabule sent for me.

'You don't want to go to Sudan?' he asked me.
'No, but I am telling you what I saw.' I replied.
'I beg, we don't continue for now.' I added.
'Don't scare the group.' he said, while pushing me away from his side.

My heart raced even faster as we came closer to the border. It was 5 a.m. when we got there.

It was an ambush. We were engulfed. I witnessed this.

It was an RPG that went off first, right in the middle. For a couple of moments, there were army legs flying everywhere, cut off from their owners. About six RPGs were dropped. I ran on my knees, both hands on the ground. I was fast. Then there were the small bullets. They tore the night apart. Rapids, singles, with interludes of bombing sounds, like perfect music to the ears. Thank God I never lost sight of Okidi. Him too. I caught him looking over his shoulder to see if I was trailing him.

However much he never showed that he cared for me before, I swear he did now.

We managed to get away. I was shot. No, the body wasn't, but the bag was leaking. It was cut and there was a splinter in the beans. The bag, not just the bag, the beans, you saved my ass.

The group was scattered. We tried to wait for the rest, but out of 208 people in the group, there were only 34 people. Okidi now took the lead. It was noon now.

Lapwony Tabule was nowhere to be seen.

The rebels planned a meeting place prior to an operation. There was always a place where we converged. We were there first. We were waiting for the rest to turn up. One hour, two hours, three. There wasn't anyone showing up. Okidi's walkie-talkie had run out of battery. No communication, just waiting for people who couldn't have made it anyway. Tension kept increasing as night neared.

At nightfall, Lapwony Tabule arrived. He had 61 people with him. Two were badly injured and were carried on a handmade stretcher.

By 9 p.m., we were 174 in total. It remained 174. The other 34 were history.

I guess nobody could even tell where the missing people were now. The bomb claimed many lives. I swear I don't know how someone who has been a soldier for four years dies in an ambush. Then look at me, only knowing how to pull a trigger, never hit a target, never even in training. The gun kept pulling me back whenever I tried to fire it.

The night was a quiet one. Lapwony Tabule sent for me the next morning. Before I got there, I could sense it wasn't friendly.

"You have juju?" he asked.

"No, I don't" I replied.

Africans, not all but the majority, believe in tradition a lot. Juju is anything that is traditional that a person has in his possession and these items are mostly believed to protect us from danger. Some people have shells, some beads, while others have bark of trees to protect them. We often spend a fortune to acquire these juju from witchdoctors.

"Tell me, then how did you know about this attack exactly?" he demanded.

I didn't have the answer and kept quiet.

It wasn't the first time strange things have happened to me. Even when I was a child, I only landed myself in trouble because of stubbornness. Something warned me.

I was stripped to my Adam suit. Everyone was watching as they searched. I had to explain every single scar on my skin. They thought it was under my skin. Well, some people did. Nothing was found. I grabbed my pants and dressed up so people didn't see me so naked.

'Don't make us suspicious again.' Tabule warned, instead of apologising.

Seriously, I wasn't expecting an apology, not from this man. Tabule had the power to make evil look holy. He was God. He had the power to make you live or die.

This was worth the shame. Everyone looked at me differently after that day. A fortune-teller or close to that. I became an asset. This opened so many doors for me, in the bush. I was protected. Even amidst attacks, Tabule never left the group before I did. I meant safety to many and this worked a bunch of times. Today, I can still sense danger.

There was nothing to explain here. Me, myself, I don't know how I did this and I still do it sometimes, today, even tomorrow.

I remember saving this group a couple of times. For example, we were eight soldiers sent on an operation to raid for foods. We polished our guns and left for the raid at sunset. We wanted to attack by 2 a.m. We were a kilometre away from the camp. I wasn't commanding the group, Okello was.

My heart raced. I thought maybe I was just tired, but it raced faster as we continued. We needed the foods. Some new recruits in the group had quite a number of days without food.

I rushed upfront to talk to our commander.

'Please cancel the operation', I begged him.

'People will get hurt.' I whispered

'How do you know that?' was his reply.

'I have a feeling that something bad is going to happen, and this isn't the first time I have had such kind of feeling' I told him.

This time, he didn't say a thing. I could see that he wanted to believe me, but what about the foods. The thoughts were written all over his face, a loyal soldier who wouldn't disappoint his superiors.

If we returned without the foods, it was obvious, countless number of whips, and no food for how many days nobody knows.

Okello halted the group suddenly. I was as surprised as the rest of the people, only that the idea was mine, so I couldn't play innocence. I had to stand to explain my hypothesis.

'We shall not attack tonight, we won't return to the group tonight', he said.

His voice was full of doubts. Even me, who came up with the idea of aborting the attack, doubted my own hypothesis.

'My boy here has something to tell you', he said as he nodded to my direction, a sign to say talk to the people. He has always called me that.

'I have a feeling there is danger ahead', I said.

'What danger?' they all asked in chorus.

'I can't tell what exactly the danger is', I replied

'But what I know is, it won't be wise to proceed with this mission', I added. They all laughed at once.

'There goes the witch doctor', one mocked me.

'So what are we going to do?' in chorus. They all came to attack me at once again.

But I could tell from both body and facial reactions, these boys were only acting brave. Their souls were scared to death.

The commander kept looking at me, head to toe. He didn't pretend.

'Shut up you people, let him explain', he confronted the boys for me.

I swear I was going to change my mind. I was not used to acting the lead role, and when I was given the opportunity, everyone seemed to notice that I was an armature.

'Let's get a safe place, spend the night, then we attack the next night', I told them.

This time, everyone was quiet; they are all looking up to the leader. The look on his face was convincing, he didn't hesitate to back me up.

That night, there were gunshots in the nearby IDP camp. Another rebel group, from a different battalion entered an ambush set by the army who were protecting the camp. The same entry route we were to take.

The following morning, bare footed, I was wearing a pair of shorts, and a sweater, not that clean. No time for laundry, especially for sweaters, they take long to dry. My hair was neat (before they forced me to make dreadlocks). I was the youngest, twelve years old. The leader sent me into the IDP camp, to observe the situation.

'My boy, don't act suspicious', he told me.

'I won't, Lapwony', I replied

'Find out how many soldiers are there, and their weapons', he added

I nodded to say, 'I won't disappoint you', as I started off to the IDP camp.

The soil felt cold to my bare feet but I was brave enough. I wanted my first mission to be a success. That was the key to another, you would always have more than plenty to eat or drink when sent out on such operations, and this was my chance. I wouldn't blow this opportunity away.

Seven of the army were out of the bush, at the roadside, all rejoicing, singing victory songs, one after another. My Swahili isn't that good or I would have dropped you a line of what they sang. My adrenaline is so easy to stimulate. I stopped. A few metres away from them, there were two dead bodies lying on the side of the road. I could tell they suffered a lot, their bodies abused. Those were my brothers; we fought together, we fought for same motives. I wanted to stand up for revenge, but then I woke up from the blackout.

I continued towards the camp. As I bypassed them, one of the soldiers grabbed a stick to hit me.

'Kids aren't allowed here', he barked at me.

I froze before him, adrenaline gathering again. I wish this man knew what I would do to him if I had my gun, or even a knife. I haven't forgiven you for the two brothers, lying on the roadside in cold blood.

He raised his hands at me. I closed both my eyes, opened them and now I am mad, from the inside.

'You dare touch me', I told him with shaky lips.

'What did you just say?' he angrily reacted.

'I don't know what you are talking about', I defended myself

'Go home before I whip you, son of a bitch', he shouted, as he brought down his stick

I took off towards the camp; I dared not to look back. Okello already told me not to act suspiciously, but I just did. Ten more soldiers were at the camp. They had one RPG, a motor, and a couple of AK47 rifles. My group only lacked a motor; we were almost square, save their number against our eight. But we are used to that.

Our superiors always told us we were outnumbered, even before starting the guerilla fighting.

This alone made us strong hearted to face any density of enemies.

I did my intelligence work well, and left the IDP camp. I reported to Okello. He didn't ask a lot of questions. Okello couldn't hide the relief I brought to his heart, I could tell from his mood that he never expected me to return. Possibly he thought I could give them to the soldiers. I managed to bag his trust that day. He couldn't hide how happy he was with the job well done, kept smiling at me whenever our eyes met.

'We are raiding the IDP camp tonight', Okello said, as we ate supper.

'These people aren't expecting any attack tonight', he added.

He deduced that well, we all believed him.

'They think they have given us quite a scare by killing two of our own', he continued

As the sun disappeared, I was ready. Everyone was quiet, attending to their only brother, sister, mother and father - that's what the guns mean to a rebel. The gun is your everything.

'Today I'm not afraid, a sign of victory', I kept singing this to myself.

I was ready, more than I have ever been before. I kept visualizing myself in the frontline as I oiled my AK47, the rifle as long as my height. The day seems not to end, and the night was longer than all I have gone through.

It was something past midnight. We set off. The closer we got to the camp, fear kept piling.

When all seemed as planned, we heard a tank just a few meters ahead. We jumped into the bush for a camouflage, the tank bypassed.

We got out, now everyone is afraid, me too, I would be a fool not to. Okello looked pale on the face.

'Stupid government', Okello spat to the ground

'We can't go back without food', he added.

We are heading to the IDP camp. I am afraid and so is everyone else. We are embarking on an unplanned mission.

Personally, I fear this place. My father was in the army. He was shot dead and buried here; I might also remain here, next to his grave, if at all they gave him a decent burial. Or I might be fed to the dogs and vultures.

It was coming to 3 a.m, we were at the outskirts of the IDP camp. We came across a man in his late twenties. We kept him in our custody, so he gave us all the vital information we needed. Then he had to direct us into the camp without anyone noticing, in exchange for his life. The shops were closed, the army patrolled the streets all night.

'*Yab dogola oyot*', Okello asked

'*In anga*?' asked a man from inside with a shaky voice

'*Abituru dogola ni kombedi*', Okello replied with ugly feelings in his voice.

The kind of voice to mean 'Don't try my patience'.

He has been so patient with this man. I know Okello, short tempered and very energetic. A man you wouldn't want to get into any physical tension with. Well, I understood where the patience was originating from that day. You couldn't confront these people, they would cause alarm and the army was metres away.

'*Ka adonyo I ot kenyo, abi neko gin mo keken ma kwo*', he roared through the key hole.

'*Omera wek ayabi*', he responded.

Okello had divided us into twos, one to watch the other's back as he looked for anything to take from the huts. World Food Programme (WFP), one of the non-government organizations operating in northern Uganda, had just distributed rations to the people at the camp two days back. We looted more than enough from the houses. It was more than we could carry and we had to abduct four more men to carry the foods.

We tied them to a single rope. Each of them had at least 100kgs to carry along, they carried everything and we never used our bullets.

I couldn't escape. I could have turned myself in to the army on the roadside when I came alone in the morning before or I could have walked up to the army patrolling the streets when Okello left me outside to watch his back while he was busy looting from the huts. But I chose not to. The leader from my village was the reason I was becoming a stonehearted killer. He knew me, he knew my family and he knew the road to my people. I was afraid he would hurt them. He often reminded me how he would enjoy slaughtering every single being I knew if I made any mistake or attempted to escape. He did this each time we met.

The most annoying part was, he called me 'brother'. Brother indeed, I wanted lightning to strike him dead, even when there wasn't a storm.

I couldn't return home, to my people, even if I had wanted to. I knew that being a rebel was changing me, now I was not afraid of killing, with a knife, gun, or even stoning you to death wasn't a problem for me any more.

From nowhere, I was a monster.

But I still carried that caring gene in me, it never went away and I had to protect my family, my people, not even sure if they are still alive. I just couldn't give Opoka the reason to hurt them. I would be someone to blame or I would blame myself for the rest of my miserable life.

All those days, weeks, months and years I spent in the bush, I had valid reasons. Sometimes I was glad I stayed longer or even much longer because, once in a while, I loved the boss life. Out there, we were the bosses. That life where you won't know what time of the day it is, not even the day of the week or the month.

We returned to the bigger group, foodstuff in plenty and four new abductees.

You don't take the items straight to your families. We converged and the items were distributed. The commanders took the best items for themselves, as though they went out there to face the enemy fetching them. They also distributed the new abductees to various families. They try to make sure the abductees never meet if possible, to avoid any escape.

It didn't take long before we were smoked out of the camp. No place is safe when you are a guerrilla fighter. I remember that morning, everybody busy lighting the fire as usual, that's the way it was done. A simple rule said, 'If you don't eat early enough, you may go without food all day'. The army might show up anytime.

That morning, a plane passed over the camp. We tried to put out the fire but it was too late. It was not a fighter plane, but one of those small passenger planes that used to pass over my village and we would scream at it, '*dege bola waraga, dege bola waraga*' literally meaning, 'aeroplane drop me a letter, aeroplane drop me a letter'. I can't remember seeing one drop a letter. Our commander decided we should stay.

Everyone had started enjoying the comfort of this camp. It was strategic, hidden from any kind of intrusion. I was getting used to my nest, I had cut grass and leaves, piled them into a heap, the length and width of a bed, then I put a polythene bag on top. Quite comfortable, yes it was because I was always there whenever I wasn't on guard duty.

The army often sent a plane to monitor the space. They particularly looked for smoke, because this would mean there are people, rebels. They would then organize a quick attack.

That day, it was so fast how they attacked. No one had finished cooking, I guess, but my family wasn't even half way with the cooking. That I knew because it was my turn to cook that day.

The guards started the shooting, while the group fled from the camp. I poured off the food, rushed to my comfortable bed to grab our solar panel. That panel had always been my responsibility. I would rather forget utensils than leave the solar panel behind.

I started chasing after the group, solar panel strapped to my back, a saucepan and jerrycan in each hand, my gun lying on my stomach. I kicked off my gumboots that were slowing me down. These army men screamed a lot, let alone yapped a lot. Most times one could cut them some slack on grounds that they were on voice training, but it got worse when they did it on your tail. Unless you wanted to give up everything, they were so dramatic there was a high chance they will eat you alive once they laid their hands on you. Trust me, you didn't want to be chased by those on the frontline despite the fact that there might be softhearted ones among them.

I dropped most of the things, they were going to make me get caught, but not the solar panel of course. I wouldn't dare. I would be sent back to fetch it or look for a replacement in exchange for my life. Without it, there wasn't communication with the other groups out there, it was used to charge batteries to the radios, sometimes we played music and danced. Yes, we did dance at the camp once. I remember I was given a very brown girl a bit older to dance with. She wasn't of my tribe, I didn't know her. I cried, I used to fear women. Even when I was back home, at school, I feared them. My teacher tried to make me sit with one in my P.4 class, I dodged school for a week and I hated the teacher so much.

There isn't anything more annoying than being shot at and you just keep running, not because you are a coward. No, they have too many soldiers and a lot better ones.

'*Mak wod pa ajwaka ni amaka*', (literally to mean 'Capture that son of a witch.') I could hear them scream after me.

I wouldn't look back. I told myself it would slow me down. I had no idea if I would find the group, just faith kept me on their heels.

'You are almost there, run, run', I told myself

I could hear my pursuers closing in, this time. From the calculation of the strides, I could tell they were two men on the chase.

'*Lalworo man ka wa maki, wabi ngoli angola calo gweno*', (meaning 'You coward, if we catch you, we will slaughter you like a chicken') one shouted.

I have never seen such determination anywhere before or thereafter.

There was a gunshot, I checked my hands for blood, didn't check the legs. They were running as before, which meant there wasn't a problem with them. There wasn't any sign of bleeding, said lots of prayers. At last I got away. They gave up.

The group ran all day, me on the trail after them. I didn't stop anywhere even when I knew they weren't pursuing me anymore.

It was sunset when I caught up with the group. We lost over twenty people in this attack, we lost most of the utensils, and all the foods were left behind. I had dropped the solar panel. No one was punished after the incident. We had a whole day of mourning at this camp, no eating or drinking water, only praying. The following day we left the camp searching for somewhere a bit safer. Not sure of the exact place, the rebels never operated much in this area, so the UPDF would not find us so easily here.

Chapter 9: Sudan

We were somewhere in the Eastern part of Uganda, had not seen the other groups for weeks. We even engaged in crossfire among ourselves. The sadness after realizing that you killed each other, your friend, the one who covered your back at frontlines, ate everyone up from the inside. We needed a proper communication, a radio and a fully charged battery each day, each moment.

I was selected. Actually I wanted in, so I went ahead and requested that I be part of the hunt even though I was not fond of this region, I felt obliged. It was my fault we lost our panel, maybe if I had stayed with the group, someone would have covered my back, but I was so slow to run with the group. Each day that we fought and found out that it was another LRA group, it went to deep in my head and I always felt responsible. I needed to return the favour. People shouldn't keep dying because it was my mistake.

Someone had to do something, and that someone was me, the victim of circumstances here. I didn't fear whether they would make me climb on top of roofs, I had that bravery I had been longing for since I was abducted.

We went for the hunt, very early in the morning, assuming most people were gone to the gardens, and the army already left after the night's watch

'Don't engage in any gun fights if possible', said Otti

Off we went. I was supposed to climb the roof that had two solar panels fastened to the roof. But there was no ladder. I couldn't manage to the top. A colleague went up in my place. It was so easy for the first panel and he sent it down. He had just started undoing the second panel, when there was gunshot. He came down the roof with a vigorous fall. He was shot in the shoulder but the arm was intact. We couldn't give him any sort of first aid, two men lifted him, I carrying the only solar panel we manage to undo from the roof. We never fought back. That's how we managed to make it back to the group.

Otti was so happy with me. He thought I was so brave. He gave me the rank of a corporal before we left for Sudan. To me it was a waste, because I would never hold that in the movement for long. To him, he was trying to convince me to stay.

The things they told us each day were so sweet to the ears. For example, they often reminded us that we would own big houses in the capital of the country once we overthrew President Museveni and his government and that we would be awarded huge ministerial posts in the new government. Those who escaped were to be punished, that is killed, with their entire families, in the new government. With all these good and horrible promises, who would think of escaping!

While out there, you totally live a lie. They often played recorded voices of people who had escaped, but those records were fabricated.

One evening, they played a recording of a girl called Sylvia. She was from our neighbouring village. She was intercepted by the UPDF from one of the attacks we had in the region.

The recording was as below;

My name is Sylvia, I escaped two days ago from LRA. My friends back there, please don't try to escape because I am about to be executed by the UPDF.

All they say on the radio about amnesty for you is not true, Please don't come back home.

With all these lies, we didn't know who to believe, but life had to go on.

Otti Vincent was the commander who led us to Sudan. The trip was very rough. Those who have been there dodged (went to other groups who weren't heading to Sudan), others even escaped to avoid going back to Sudan.

I didn't want to go there either, because I was told what a terrible place it was. I don't want to go to my own grave, that's what they used to refer to Sudan.

As if I had a choice. Escape was out of contention at the moment, though I thought about it. I wanted to believe whatever they planted into my head. Sometimes, these people didn't seem too bad. They had hearts too. I witnessed that on several occasions when told to ferry injured comrades from the frontlines

We had a week to prepare, as the days kept counting down. The options kept vanishing and finally, I had none. The journey started. We spent nearly six days trekking with a lot of difficulties, walking long distances, hunger, cold and carrying heavy loads. We fought the UPDF each day, changed routes more than three times to get across the border. Very many people, close friends and not such close ones died or were injured. I always survived because those who I was assigned to were good people. They made sure I was in sight.

We got there. In the south of Sudan, grasses are at the height of my knee, no tall trees, only thickets and shrubs, such a barren land. Both my heels blistered. I made myself an improvised crutch, using forked tree trunks. I said a thousand prayers to make it to this place. Just like all those who have been to this place say, Sudan isn't a place to be. It's the true wilderness described in the Holy Bible. The wind too dry to inhale, too much heat, but the nights extremely cold. Most of us didn't have a blanket, or bed sheets. We slept close to a campfire, even that wasn't warm enough to keep you warm the whole night.

When we had reached Sudan we were divided into different groups and I was personally allocated to a group headed by Kony and his senior commanders.

Here, we new recruits didn't really actively participate in military missions. It was like home. No one came to attack our camp, and the Sudanese government supplied us with foodstuffs, guns and bullets for some reasons only the top commanders knew. Kony and his commanders embarked on serious farming in Sudan and we were the labour force. Just like the prisoners, they used to send us to the farms as early as six in the morning, and there was someone supervising. You were never allowed to stand up.

One day we were out in the field, I still vividly recall this event. We were digging in a large farm, it was afternoon already, we hadn't had anything to eat and a girl digging next to me hit a landmine. It could have been in the soil for years. There was a blast, and the whole place was covered in dust. There she was, a girl aged about 13 years, lying in a pool of blood, unconscious. She lost her hand, injured her left eye badly, without a doctors' examination, one could tell that the eye was gone. The abdomen was a mess, her intestines were hanging out covered in soil. I still can't deduce how they weren't cut. The intestines were intact and she was breathing. Kony ordered she should be rushed to Khartoum Hospital. Only God knows what transpired thereafter for her. I never saw her again

Yes I made it to this horrible place, but why do I have the feeling that I won't make it out of here? I have all the right to think that, in a place with no food or water, movement aided with an improvised crutch. If I go out there and look for food and water, I won't survive.

I wrote a suicide note;

*The minds that are prevented from changing their opinions, they cease to mind.
I am sorry mother, it can't work this way.*

I knew mother wouldn't get the letter, but it lifted lots of burdens from my heart. I kept the letter in my pocket, had wanted to do it when the night falls, prayed to God for forgiveness and to clear my path. I didn't want to suffer anymore.

Whenever I wanted to vanish from the face of the earth, I always seemed to end up in the woods. I had wanted to die the first time I set foot in Sudan, whenever I got the chance. Just like being in a movie set, there is always a surprise around the corner and it's always booming with couple of amazing characters.

In this, my movie as it seems, the amazing character was a random boy, two years older than I was. We really didn't share our stories that much. All we knew about us was it was our first time in Sudan. He talked a lot; I liked his company, even if we were total strangers. We were sent to fetch water from a stream. As usual, you only bathe when they sent you to the stream. Most of the times, you were pre-occupied; bathing had never been a priority to a rebel. We filled our cans, and decided to bathe. This friend pushed me into the water, just before I could remove all my clothes. My suicide letter was ruined, but that didn't change a thing. I wanted to die, but then the water became nice. I walked out of it, pretended as though nothing was going on. Then before he could realize, my friend went flying into the water. I had pushed him just like he did to me. It was fun in the water; I didn't want him to miss this. For about 30 seconds, he wasn't anywhere to be seen. I got scared, and concerned, he sprung to the surface, his belly almost distended to maximum. He had swallowed whole loads of water; I jumped to give him a hand just before he vanished again beneath the waters. I grabbed him by his arm and dragged him to a shallower side of the stream.

For me, I love the reaction on people faces. I live for that. Everybody reacts differently, sometimes they laugh, sometimes they are shocked, some people even get scared but there is always one moment I look at them and I see a glint in their eyes and for that second, believe that anything is possible. And I can testify to that, when I saw how terrified my friend was, I knew God never wanted me dead. I was afraid too. I sat down with my friend; we both cried when I told him what I wanted to do. We both decided to realize how special our lives were and we headed back to the camp, my heart as light as I needed.

We can create something extraordinary, with the most ordinary people. Sometimes it's the things we don't expect which are the most powerful. How was I supposed to know that a simple water game, which actually failed because my friend couldn't swim, could change the way I look at things, the way I think. Well, it's something I didn't expect that saved my life.

I woke up and it was coming to dawn. I dashed to the nearby bush. Had I delayed for a minute, I would have defecated in my pants. It took me about ten minutes to come out of the bush, but before I got out, I could feel the regrouping in my belly. I made three heaps. Honestly, they weren't heaps, they looked like a water body.

The population at the camp became enormous, without a clean water source, no latrine, it didn't take long before the bushes couldn't hold our dung anymore. The hygiene of the camp wasn't the best. A lot of people died of cholera at this camp. The Sudanese government tried to give some help, but the prevalence was too much to be contained. They decided to quarantine all of us who had cholera. They abandoned us one kilometre away from the camp. They could bring us some food once a day, of course not enough for everyone. Most of the food was often poured onto the ground as we struggled to have our share. There wasn't any form of treatment, we were meant to die. The guards watched us from a distance to make sure no one escaped from the valley of death. Each morning, they brought new ones who contracted cholera and took away the dead bodies.

I ate a lot of soil, I thought it would harden my diarrhoea. Luckily, there was this nice guy I always talked to, about the things to do to survive. He was in his late twenties and had already been in the bush for eight years. He never had any intention to leave it and often called the bush his home.

He could steal some medicines and brought them to me in the nights, when everyone was asleep, until the diarrhoea stopped. He asked that I be brought back to the camp, taking care of me until I was back to my feet.

When I managed to get back to my feet, I was selected into a group that was to lead us back to Uganda. The Khartoum government wasn't on good terms with us anymore. The Arabs had started fighting and they didn't want us there. They had better weapons, foods; they were good both on land and in the air. They thought the LRA wanted their oil. In Uganda, UPDF activities became so intense, with every community joining hands to fight the LRA. The eastern region had the *Arrow boys*, the northern region had the *Acholi okeco* and the Lango region had the *Amuka*.

Life became very rough with constant attacks all day and night with no rest; they smoked us from all the hideouts you could think of whenever we stayed in one campsite for more than a night.

These people gave all they had to protect their communities. They were never paid a single coin. It was just a service to the community, the one thing the UPDF had almost failed to do. The sad note is that, they perished in huge numbers to the rebels. They were annoying, our own brothers and sisters fighting us and they had to die so that they learned that we were not a joke. Not just anyone could put up a fight against us. These people never received any kind of training, just like all of us, but we had the experience, we had been doing this for ages. They were meant to supply us with foods and information to bring down the government, now they turned their back at us.

They forced us to do things we regret up to now, things like:

This seems odd to many. We were told, forced to believe, and enforced that Fridays were sacred. Go to your shamba (farm) on a Friday, don't let us find you working. Those who thought it was a joke, they can testify. Well, it may sound unfair to many, especially the non-Muslims. So many people fell victims of this order. I remember one day

Lapwony Vincent Otti gave orders for an operation. We were between the hills so it was a very good hideout, very strategic with a fine view of an intruder before he noticed you.

He gathered everyone at the parade yard. It was a chilly morning, fog covered the hills and I was grinding my teeth against each other with the cold, my gun standing tall next to me.

'The people here have failed to listen to the orders, so we shall teach them a lesson today', Otti started

'Carry your machetes. Any Acholi who doesn't follow orders has waged war against us', he added

No one asked a question. He picked the crew himself. They were eleven. I wasn't part of this team. He laid them to the ground and hit them fifteen pangas to the back to raise their adrenaline.

'You go out there and do just what I did to you or more, no mercy for stubbornness', he concluded with rage in his eyes, as he sent the team out running.

When they returned, their uniforms soaked in blood, we weren't told anything, but the radio told us. 21 people had their limbs amputated; some lost both legs while others lost the arms.

Since the incident, it wasn't possible to find a soul digging on a 'sacred' Friday, others even confessed that Thursdays were to near to Fridays and they wouldn't dare make such a mistake.

The same thing went for bicycle riding. The LRA, for no good reasons, abolished the use of bicycles. Some thought the local people got away a lot faster with bikes than on foot. Once you were found riding, you were accused of trying to run away. Yet the LRA claimed they were working for the better of the Acholi people, who in turn were trying to abandon them. The punishment for having a bicycle in your home, let alone riding it, is they smash the bicycle first, before crippling you. It was absurd but the Acholi people learnt to live with such cruelty from their own children. The problem with this war was the parents always condemned the army instead of themselves who, at some point, should stand up and take responsibility. Once a kid was taken by the LRA, all we did was freak out, visualizing all sorts of horrible things. Yes, there were horrible things, but not all I went through while out there was horrors. I admit that I enjoyed a couple of occasions as well as suffering most of the time. When a parent freaked out because rebels came asking for information or foods, what would you do? Our parents didn't care about themselves anymore. They gladly gave the rebels their foods and any information they asked for. They were only doing this to protect their child who is taken, hoping that one day he returns, but not knowing they are strengthening the force.

His death was a gift, well, sort of; I know you won't understand it.

Tinka, my old friend, got shot by the Dinka people.

I was left behind at the camp. I was on guard, watching over the camp while they went on a raid. Losing my friend brought me into my full reality.

I faced my deepest fears. I had complete awareness that nothing can hurt me now.

Chapter 10: Escape

The escape wasn't beautiful at all. It took us two weeks to get out of the bush. I must admit that we lost, however much I made it back home. Eight survived, we bludgeoned one to death, two were slaughtered by UPDF soldiers, one was bitten by a snake and one taken by the river. These things you will only do when you are out of your senses, but when you are tired of being a killer, you will always chose to get killed.

We wanted as many guns as possible. We managed six, but the other seven had no guns. But the determination, the trust and a team were all we needed. We buried the guns in sand at a shamba half a mile away from a camp. We failed to start the escape journey three times. Each time we tried, there was something blocking our way, the last being the most dreadful.

He was one of us. He suddenly changed his mind, he wanted to go back to the camp, he was carrying a gun and fear overtook him.

'Put down all the guns', he ordered. He was the last man at the back

We stopped, turned to see it was him.

'I said put down the guns or I will shoot whoever has one', he added

'Come on, what do you think you are doing?' one asked.

'Shut up, nobody talks, just do as I say', he barked

We laid all the five guns in front of him, he gathered them closer to him using his feet, while pointing his gun at us.

'Everybody stay calm, nobody gets hurt', he kept talking as he managed to get all the guns to himself.

'Please don't do this to us', I begged

'You will get us killed', I added

'I will be promoted for turning you traitors in. Do you have any idea how cool that is', he bragged.

'Everybody turn around. We are going back to camp, where we belong', he shouted, his gun still pointing at us.

'Let's go, nobody looks back', he yelled, leading us back to the camp

'Brother, if you don't want to escape, please let us go' another man begged

He halted us, to a stop under a huge tree. The guy wanted to tie us up to a rope and then to the tree

'I'll leave you guys here as I rush to report, ha ha ha', he laughed mockingly, while making a knot on his rope, gun strapped to his shoulder.

'I can jump on him', one whispered

'Don't be stupid, can't you see he will shoot all of us', a man next to me replied in a shaky voice.

'I said quiet', our only enemy shouted

'I need your support guys, we can bring him down', one of us whispered.

He finished making knots on his rope. The man came to tie us up to the tree.

'Everybody keep calm, else you will see blood', he threatened

He started with the only girl in the group, she never resisted. When our eyes met, the look in her eyes said it all. She blamed me for the incident. Well, it could be my fault but I didn't force anybody to join the escape. Dear little girl, I feel sorry for all of us, but that doesn't mean I am to blame.

The one jumped on him, they all went rolling over the little girl

'Take the gun, take it', he shouted

I grabbed the gun by the magazine. He held onto the gun, the magazine came off. I had the bullets. He had the gun. He lost the battle; he gave up because we were too many.

'Ok, ok, ok, let's talk', he shouted

"There is nothing to discuss my friend", one of us shut him up.

This new leader was a strange person, unpredictable. He was the commander now.

'Let's kill him, the bastard asked for it', he ordered

Well, this was no surprise. Anybody, if asked to make a call of judgment, would do the same. Let this man have a taste of his own will, yes, that's his wish for all of us.

The one who had disarmed him started by clubbing this man on the neck right from behind, I followed by hitting him at the back of the head using the butt of my gun. When the last person reached his turn, the man was into dust, totally unrecognizable. He was scared, we were too, but he was more. He were strong enough; brave enough, otherwise we wouldn't make it back home. We had to do it.

Sometimes mercy betrays us, mercy makes us weak and vulnerable.

How he cried for mercy. I used to picture him in my sleep.

We were back on track. My prayer was that no one changes their minds like that man did. We had to walk and run at the same time to cover the time that fool wasted.

We had run out of supplies three days ago. You could see that everyone was losing stamina, the balance was not there anymore. We were twelve a week ago, two days later, we were nine and on this very day we were eight, maybe the following day we wouldn't have had anyone to write this book. We decided to walk less, while keeping an eye open for anything edible. A number of rats became our prey, some lizards, crocodiles were victims of circumstances. Since then I have believed you can eat anything. Lots of people would think lizards or crocodiles are normal foods, but for the Acholi people, they are taboo. I wouldn't ever eat with you in the same room if I got to know that you touched a reptile with your bare hands.

Chapter 11: Leopards

We came to a cave, not far away from a water source, a salty stream that had stopped flowing probably weeks ago. All the animals came to quench their thirst here, a strategic place to exercise our hunting skills. We want the water, too, maybe its saltiness will get us back to the road home. I initiated the escape, designed the plans and plotted all the possible exit routes to take on a piece of paper that was in my head, without telling anybody. You just couldn't bring such a conversation to anyone. There were specific people you chose to share your brilliant ideas with. Even with that, you were fifty-fifty uncertain they wouldn't turn you in.

At first I wanted to do it alone. Yes, the great escape plan was mine and mine alone. But then I thought of the rivers, the snakes, the lions, hostile tribes on the way and the army on your tail. How was I to encounter all these possible calamities? That turned out be a suicide mission, not an escape mission. I had to involve twelve more soldiers to execute this plan. They all had to take an oath before involving themselves. Just like breaking out of a prison, some will always die to save the rest.

We found two leopard cubs in the cave. It was the best meal I had after a long time, even though there was no salt. We sat down, relaxing after the huge meal. The big cat returned, from a hunt I suppose. She sat at the entrance of the cave with her butt on the ground, the two front legs firmly supporting her. In her eyes, you could see rage. She wanted her young ones. We all froze, she jumped at the one girl, tore her dress, and gave her a long scratch from the face to the stomach before the cat dashed out, and the girl was bleeding all over. It was so stupid of us, no one put up a fight to bring down the big cat. She didn't take long. She was back, with a male companion now.

Our problem was doubled. This wouldn't have happened if we all had stood up to confront the female leopard while she was alone. Now we had to face the reality. I looked around and the fear in my friends' eyes told me that there really was a problem.

'Load the gun' I told one boy.

At least he managed to hold his. Most of us were too shaky to grab ours. He took the female with one bullet, the male freaked out for a moment. Just before we settled for a victory, he was there, standing at the entrance of the cave, all claws and teeth bared. He took him down too, another single shot. We didn't have enough bullets, so we promised never to miss a shot.

'You rather fail to fire than miss a target', we had agreed.

We had a lot to eat, so we ate until what remained could be carried along. We had taken a while without such a meal. Putting aside the injuries sustained, the experience was wonderful.

While others thought we should kill her, for a moment I thought the injured girl was a burden too, but when I remembered that I was escaping to nourish my soul, I was only too happy to help whenever it was my turn. We all carried this girl on a stretcher in turn. We didn't have any medicine, she only had wild herbs to treat the wounds and she was doing so well until we got out of the bush.

'I know this place', one of the boys said confidently.

'Are you sure', another boy asked

'Yes, I grew up here.' he mentioned confidently.

'Well, we shall hide the guns, then you will go to look for the Local Councilor's house', one of us said.

'You bring him here, he will then take us to the barracks', he added.

We all freaked out at the sound of a barracks. No one was sure it was a good idea. We were told the army never spared anyone returning from the bush

The boy changed to civilian clothes and off he vanished, only to return with an old man, not the LC. The old man said everyone had abandoned the village and he had only come to look for food from the gardens.

He was a good man. He gave us lots of raw cassava to eat on our way to the barracks, with him leading the way. We passed through the IDP camp, people gathered along the route to see us. You could tell from the look on their faces, they were searching for their loved ones who were once taken and had not showed up yet, others had accusing looks all over the faces.

I remember walking through this crowd with my head down most times.

I couldn't take the blame, for the things I was forced to do. Anyone can kill once told to do it. We were never just told to kill. We were forced. Nothing we were told back there was true or good.

We had a warm welcome by the army at the barracks, were given pair of scissors to shave our hair and water to clean up and were treated to a nice meal together with the commanders at the barracks. The following day, one of us led them to where we buried the guns, before being transferred to a big barracks in Kitgum district. Here, the army was friendly for all the three days we were waiting to be sent to the rehabilitation centre.

I hated this place, everyone looked the same, it was like joining another LRA group, the boys and girls always did the things I am trying to run away from. In the dormitories, you found a clique of boys trying to bully those who just arrived. They often demanded respect, yet it was against the policy of the centre, the administrators said so.

I felt new, but every day I did the same things. I ate the same things at the same time at the same table. I was terrified of confinement.

One morning, I sat on my bed here at the rehab centre and I ate my breakfast, couldn't help thinking of what the future held for me when I got back home. None of my family members visited me, all the one month I was here.

That created a lot of tensions within me. I was not sure if they were still alive or if they could have visited. I ended up losing my appetite. These thoughts wanted me to starve to death, I guess. They only clouded my mind whenever I had anything to eat. You know, the routine: visitors came, we danced, sang for them, they briefed us – each day. I had these tracks I always ran on, that changed me. I could make new tracks. But the things in my life, the things in my past, they are not resolved. They need to be attended to. I am leaving this rehab center to look for my family and then my journey can truly begin.

It's easy to act tough but difficult to assume the consequences. They begged me to stay a little longer at the rehab centre. I wanted to, but there were so many things running in my mind, the questions that needed answers, not just answers but urgent answers. My head could have exploded had I stayed here any longer. This place was a place of wide lawns and narrow minds, especially talking to those children who were born and raised in the movement (from the bush).

The things they did in the dormitories leave someone wondering if both sides of the brains were working.

They won't understand a single thing. They won't change.

Chapter 12: Coming home

I love the way true astonishment can even make a grown man feel like a kid again. I was twelve years old, but inside, I was a man. She was there standing at the granary, her head was inside but the whole body was outside. Mother was trying to pull out some sorghum.

'Olango, Olango, Olango', shouted my young brother.

'Olango is back.' he added, running to collect me from the road.

'Stop there, don't move a step forward', mother shouted from the granary. She pushed the top of the granary away and jumped down to see what was happening

'My Olango, is that you?' she cried

'Yes mother, it's me, your Olango', I replied.

I was crying, she was crying.

My brother was laughing; he thought I brought something for him to eat. I was surprised he never forgot my face. He was a toddler when I was taken.

'Stand still, let me come', she added as she dashed to the house

In no time, she was back, with an egg in her hand; she placed it in the middle of the path right in front of me.

'Step on it before stepping into my compound', she said. This is a form of ritual the Acholi people do when welcoming someone they expected never to meet again

I did step on the egg, it broke beneath my foot and I moved into the compound. She was crying all this time. As if that wasn't enough, she had to carry me on her back as if I was a two year old kid. She took me to the house, never asked me anything about the bush.

2004 was special to me. It was my rebirth. I was lost but now am found. Everyone I met on the road seemed to have seen a ghost. They often looked back until I was gone.

Once in a while, I often heard them say my name in a conversation I didn't even know.

Even the best dancer in the world can look crazy to those who can't hear the music. It was so bad to my ears to hear them talk at my back, as if I had wished for the abduction. I had nothing to offer anybody but my own confusion because I didn't understand why the world was so cruel to some people and it's very romantic with others.

In awful dreams, I found myself appearing in the most amazing places, sometimes in the most horrible places, doing the things I always did while back there. I would scream in my nightmares, I fought all sorts of wars in my sleep, winning some and getting killed in a few. I would mimic all types of sounds of guns each time I went to bed. Well, I don't know if that's true, but the people I slept with said so.

I have to admit that this journey through my story has been full of surprises. I regret many, but the truth is I would have a different take on life, one that was not the one my family offered. Those surprises, you don't expect them coming.

All I care is that life is the greatest gift.